to all of the kids who were told
"just get over it"
this is for you…

I have burns
        From fires
I never started

I have bruises
        from punches
I never threw

I have scars from knives
I drew on myself
out of feeling like a
Failure

Growing up
I was taught that love is
measured
by how much
you spend on the person.
I grew up…
And didn't get much from my S.O.
So I assumed I was
Unlovable.

They say people who are hurt…
           hurt others.
Then explain to me
       why I have been hurt
by everyone who was "supposed" to love me.
Yet…
 I treat everyone
        better than I treat
                       myself.

I have learned how to mask.
How to put on this smile that hides what's really
happening.
I was told by everyone - that didn't happen.
That isn't true.
Stop lying.
Then why are the
Nightmares are real,
The scars are present,
and the texts are still in the cloud.

I am always asked why I doubt myself.
Well…

       Because they said, "that never happened".
But it did.
Years later he came forward.
I was questioned for hours and hours.
Lost friends and family.
But 4 years later you think you can come forward..
Say sorry.
And it'll heal
      the damage,
      the shakes,
      the scars,
      the tears,
      the wet pillows,
      the broken frames,
      the broken self.
You get to live while I am still suffocating under your
hand.

Relationships.
That fun word.
The word that is supposed to bring you joy.
All it has brought me is tears.
On my cuffs.
On my pillows.
Not on anyone's shoulder…
because
"it didn't happen"

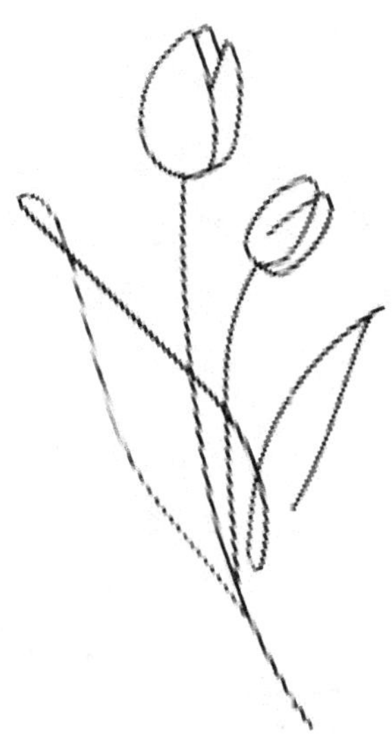

You.
You told me
    I am crazy.
    I am a liar.
    That I can't be trusted.
I ask myself
    What's wrong with me?
    I swear I saw that…
    I swear he said that…

I sit here in this 2 hour session. Realizing that
You
You.
        Were the problem.
            The cheater
            The heartbreaker
            The liar
            The user.
        Not me.
I gave,
you took…
        More than I had to offer.

There are indents on my steering wheel.
Where I used to grip on hard because I
convinced myself you were following me.
I felt crazy.
I knew it was you.
You are the darkness
The shadow that is in the corner of my room
You are the depression,
The meds I take,
to try to get rid of.

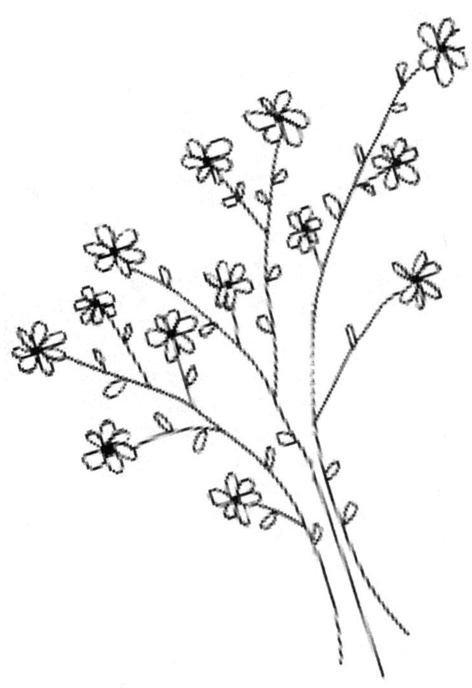

My therapist stares at me long and hard and asked…
Why are you so scared of failing?
Because I failed at love.
With my friends.
My family.
Myself.

Yet I was never loved the same.

So I am terrified to fail at anything else.
Especially,
when I failed myself.

But that wasn't you that
failed them.

They
failed
you…

What am I really scared of?

Scared that no one can understand
the trauma I have been through.
No one can understand the
hurt I have witnessed.
How I learned to love.
How I learned to heal.
How to cope.
How to hide.
I am terrified I can't be loved.
I can't be fixed.
I
Am
Broken.

I have believed my entire life,
All of the trauma I experienced
was meant to happen to me.
Cause, "everything happens for a reason".
I was told that,
I deserve to be hurt.
I deserve to feel pain.
I don't deserve happiness.

Why is it
the ones who hurt us the most
are the ones who
stay in our minds the most.

My family always said to share what you are feeling.

Yet would spread it to everyone who was in sight.

Would also tell you "not appropriate"

So

How am I supposed to share what I am feeling,
if everyone will know.

Maybe this is why I hold EVERYTHING in.
And eventually just explode.
I get asked,
Why are you so angry about the fork in the sink?
It's not the fork…
or the sink…
It's the things that went unsaid.

I only know how to muffle,
How to hide,
How to hide the cries at night.

Never let them know,
How you truly feel.

I only know how to hide,
How to hold the secret,
How to hold in the things that happened.

Never let them think,
That they know what the truth is.

Because they don't know.
They never will.
And if they do,
They won't listen.

Because "that never happened"

Wipe. Wipe the tears that never were meant to cry.
Cry the tears that should only be let out for deaths
and love.
Cry the tears that shouldn't be happening.
But wipe.
Hide.
Don't let them see.
The true tears that you cry,
Cry yourself to sleep,
Because no…
This isn't normal.
Holding my pillow to muffle the cries and the screams.
To wipe away the pain you gave me.
The pain no one understands.
The darkness.
The light.
No matter how much I try.
I can't wipe the tears that were never meant to cry.

There's a blade.
A sharp blade that,
Pierces the skin.

Not the skin you own.

But the skin that is damaged.

You don't own this skin anymore.
It has shed.
Maybe if I use this blade enough.
The only bruises I will have…
Are from me…
But not me.
The me that wasn't taken away when you hurt me.
When you pinned me down.
When you told me to stop talking, screaming, crying.
When you held me against my will.

On my childhood bed.

Yes it did happen.

Yes I won't forget.

And yes, you did do it.

I hope you trust me.
I hope you believe me.
I shouldn't have to beg an officer, to stop asking,
Over,
Over,
And,
Over, again.

Yes it did happen.
Yes I have proof.

Years later.
I see you.
You see me.
"Sorry"
I can't breathe.
I can't think.
I'm back. At the spot you left me.
Where I changed.
Where I'll never be the same.
"I'm sorry… I didn't know better".

How is it that you get to be okay,
While I struggle everyday.
When I was asked over,
Over,
And, over,
Yes. it did happen.
With no "yes's" involved.

But now you and I are the only ones
who knows the truth.
It was you. You and only you.

I need help.
Please help me.

That never happened.
What were you wearing?
How short were your shorts?
You were asking for it.
She's LYING.

Did this actually happen?
Did this actually happen?

Did,
This,
Actually happen?

Yes. I promise you. It did.

Smack.

Bang.

Crash.

I love you.

Smack.

Bang.

Crash.

I'm sorry.

Smack.

Bang.

Crash.

I love you.

Smack.

Bang.

Crash.

It's okay.

You are the problem.
You ar e the problem.
You a r e the problem.
You a r e n the problem.
You a r e n t the problem.

You aren't the problem.

Can you hold me?
Can you tell me that I was right?
I need you to know, these things… they did happen.
They aren't a movie,
A book,
A story.
They are your story.
And you have
EVERY
Right.
To share them.
Scream them.
Yell them.
Feel them.

You deserve to know you aren't the problem.

The scars on my arm are from me.
The scars on my arm are not from me.

They are because I don't deserve to be hurt.
They are because I deserve to be hurt.

They are there to remind me I'm still alive.
They are there to remind me I'm "damaged goods".

They are there because I gave up on myself.
They are there because everyone gave up on me.

But really
They are my battle wounds.
They continue show me how low I was,
and what I fought
That rock bottom does have a basement.
But I am still here for a reason.

PREVIEW of NEW Book:

I thought it was normal
to wake up to
screaming
in the middle of the night.
That it was normal to wear ear plugs
and act like it was just the TV.
That the yelling was just the neighbor's..
until I grew up and realized.
No.
That isn't "normal".